I0140399

INCENTIVE

INCENTIVE

Ellen Higgins

INCENTIVE

Copyright © Ellen Higgens, 2019

All rights reserved. No part of this publication may be reproduced, stored in a retrieval system, or transmitted in any form or by any means, electronic, mechanical, photocopying, recording, or otherwise, without written permission of the author and publisher.

Published by Ellen Higgins, Edmonton, Canada

ISBN   978-1-77354-101-3 Print
        978-1-77354-101-3 eBook

Publication assistance and digital printing in Canada by

PAGEMASTER
PUBLISHING
PageMaster.ca

Contents

I am not smart, but I love to observe: the love of missionaries.

At the age of 16, I got to know my missionaries Andrea and her husband Chet A. Lowe, through Calvary chapel church in Buchanan. Sis Andrea Lowe was a loving and caring woman of God who lived in Florida. They were missionaries in my home town, of Buchanan in Grand Bassa county.

They came from the United States of America to spread the word of God to many Liberians when the civil war ended for a period of time.

From age 7 to 16 I was one of the faithful members in the St Peter Catholic Church Buchanan. I was born January 31, the same birthday as my pastor son Micaiah. While growing up as a teen, I decided that I wanted to become one of the Catholic sister (nun) due to the influence of the dress code, respectfulness towards kids, their way of teaching in school and encouragement, influence me to become a Catholic sister. However, my dad really wanted me to become a Catholic sister in the family. Which I agreed to.

Growing up in the Catholic church I had no idea that god was going to lead me to a Christian church which I knew for sure he no longer wanted me to be in the Catholic church again.

After been in the Catholic church for so long as a kid, God showed me where he wanted me to be and learned his true words. And it was Calvary Chapel Church.

Visiting Calvary chapel bible study the first time in the year 1995, and listening to brother Chet teaching, about baptism of the holy spirit, on that faithful month of September, in church, amazed me.

At that moment, I made up my mind to become a Calvary chapel member. Because his teaching was a true doctrine.

After preaching, he said if anyone of you want to get baptize, please write your name on the sheet of paper. I wrote my name that day for baptism. The day that change my story into glory. I can never forget this day. I felt so special and grateful when I place my name on the sheet to become a born again Christian.

When I got baptized on that faithful Saturday, a tremendous excitement hit me like never before. Because I was hungry for God and whatever he had to offer. I was a perfect example of being thirsty and hungry according to his glory.

When I got baptized and came home that Saturday morning, mom noticed something different on me, she noticed my hair was wet, I had a big towel and different clothes on.

Mom was cooking that day when I came home after I got baptized. She began to ask me where did I go and how come I am wet. I explain to her that I got baptized in a new church call Calvary chapel up Christian high school area. She was so mad at me and said that she will tell my dad about what I did . By not telling her that I was going to be baptized on that day. I got baptize into a river near a park. I got baptize without my parents consent. I realized what I should have done in the first place was to invite my parents to my church before getting baptized. But I was also unhappy with dad telling me that my new church was not a good church so I got afraid to tell them. At that time, dad had travel to Monrovia so I took the opportunity to do things on my on as a teen.

The painful part of my story:

Here comes my dad back from Monrovia, the capital city of Liberia. My loving country. The country that put God first in bad or good situation. The citizens of Liberia are obsessed with Christianity no kidding. Now when my dad came back home, the news reached him that I got baptized without my family members. Oh my God, I was in total trouble.

I was worried and in fear that my dad will beat me and punish me as well. Well I could not do anything about it. I was waiting on my punishment. First of all, I been use to dad beating me and punishing me anyways. It is part of the culture. And dad used to explain to us that he came up the hard way while living with his uncles and extended relative who treated him mean. Anyways I got my punishment, and was beaten as well. However I was strong and did not give up.

Dad was so mad until he said that he wanted to show his butt to brother Chet. Everyone in our yard begin to laugh. Dad was so funny. My dad got mad and said that I have to go back to the Catholic church because I was a child when I began a Catholic and I promised him that I wanted to become a Catholic nun.

Of course I said that but when I grew up, I realized that my decision was wrong. So I changed my mind and wanted to have my own kids when I get married. Secondly, when I heard the requirement of been a nun, it discourage me not to go into it anymore. because I wanted to have kids.

I tried to explain my reason to dad, but he refused to listen to me. I told dad I did not want to be a Catholic nun for the rest of my life. I needed to have my own kids. I believed life is all about boldness and also standing up for yourself. When issued like bullying take place in your life.

He said that my church was not a good church but 666 church. Ha ha OMG Dad was so funny. He always make us laugh every day at home and places. Dad is truly a comedian. No kidding I am serious.

Now the serious bullying part on my story is about to take place:

After I got punished, beaten, and calling me some kinds of names, you know how our African parents do things right, my dad stopped me from going to worship in my church. Can you imagine how painful it is. After going through all those embarrassment in front of your siblings and relatives, then out of a sudden, you are not allowed to go to your church anymore. All because I decided to changed my faith and philosophy. I did not relent or force my way out by disrespecting him at all. But was hurt inside. No kidding!

Everyday I make sure to do my house chores for my parents. I never hold any grudges against my parents. All I did, was to stand on my word to not become a Catholic sister anymore.

I was a very happy kid, did not worry about dad's bullying me about my church. I knew things were going to change around for my own good. So I play low by keeping quite.

Until one day, after six months, a lady from our church, saw my dad in front of our house and told my dad that you have a beautiful daughter. From one thing to another Calvary chapel name came about. The lady told dad the church was great church and dad should allowed me to take part in the church activity and grow in the things of God. And it is a very good church that teaches God's words and keep kids from being part of bad influences in the community.

She was an angle sent by God to make my dad to understand that I was making the right decision. When she got through talking with dad, he call me inside the house and apologized for what he did to me. I excepted his apology and said thanks and appreciate his kindness towards me by apologizing.

Apparently, Dad understood me and apologized for keeping me for the past 6 months at home. And cooperating with me to make my own choice when it comes to my faith and the church I want to worship. I knew it was an important step for me and did not stop worshiping my god in the church. For me it was all about the church sermons, and the love of the praise and worship songs.

Thanks be to God that I changed my decision and took the bold step of following a different philosophy that opened my eyes to the truth and an honest way of following Christ.

The enjoyment part of my church Calvary Chapel:

Now I am on the move to explain my real life story.

After been told to not step foot to my church for 6 months, I was allowed by my dad to go back to my loving and caring church. I was so happy to go and meet all my friends and pastors, play mom, and missionaries again when I went back to my church, everyone were so excited to see me again. And I was also excited to see them as well.

Now I began a full members of Calvary chapel, join the choir and join the kick ball team as well. Calvary chapel Liberia ministry, was one of the greatest ministries I ever love and believed as a youth.

It was one of the ministries that taught me how to love others and be caring to your neighbor and friends and family.

Our missionaries were caring and nice people in Buchanan those days. They were loving and friendly people I spent most of my time with in Liberia (Grand Bassa county).

These couples inspired me a lot while growing up with them. For this reason, I wanted to be an example of them. Begin around them for so long, I got used to them till up to this day. I don't know why, but got inspired with their relationship as a teenager girl.

This is the funny part of this story:

Those days we used to have our bible study on the football field with my friends Mardea, sister Marconi, sister grace, and many others near their house. There were lots of fun activities, such as baseball, football, volleyball and so on. It was fun playing together with different kids in their back yard and the church members.

The good thing about after playing all day, we always had food ready at the Lowe's house for everyone whether a church members or not. There were always enough food during the play period. The funny part of this story is that boys in our community were football players. And you know how football players love to eat lots of rice after playing their games back home. Ha ha, and second it was free food. Ha ha those days.

Whenever, these guys heard that we are having kick ball and football games, they know that they will eat until their belly burst. Ha ha. What a beautiful time together those days. Secondly, these guys were looking for their wife to be in the church and community.

So whenever they are coming, they will dress up in their best clothes just to confused those girls. It was really fun and serious acting those days. Young boys them. Ha ha. Our cook was Sis Grace. She was a very great cook. I always used to tell her that she was the best cook in the whole wide world. That was my motivation . She was a very strong woman who work so hard, never complain of been tired of cooking everyday for others.

Getting up early morning and putting those big pots on the fire, to cook for hundreds of people, in a day time, was a great challenge for woman like her. Very clean and neat. I love you Sis Grace .My prayers is to have you visit me in Canada to see me and my family one day. You are like a mother to me now no matter what, you deserved more from me. You treated me like your own and took me from hunger. Not that I was homeless, but you took me to be your daughter among the entire group of girls in Calvary chapel.. For this reason, I have kept you in my heart for so long to help you come to Canada. This has been my prayers for so long since I came to Canada. I am sorry Sis Grace for not fulfilling my promise. You were so patient, wise woman of God and treated everyone like your own kids.

During those days, with lots of boys living with the Lowe's, over 20 people, to set and cook for them without complaining amazed me. What a kind-heated woman.

She was a role model for others like us and she set example for many children, friends and family by showing them love, and caring dedication and commitment she did for her own Liberians and the Lowe's family.

My next favorite pastor:

My next favorite pastor was Sammy. He was one of the football players those days. He was tough on us as a teen and members in the church to be bold and tell him who we were dating those days. So funny. But he was a very nice guy. I can remember, one Saturday afternoon, we were call for a meeting by our pastor (Sammy).

The meeting was arranged to ask everyone of us who were members and had position in the church, about our relationship those days. All of us in the music department, like Evon, Prince, Mardea, Joe Marks Brother Lawrence, Austin, Sis Nancy, Albertine, Celestine, and Emmanuel Duah, and Brother Daniel and brother Flanpor who were Calvary chapel teachers and so on came for the meeting.

The meeting begin and it was time for us to be bold and say the truth. After chatting and greeting each other, our pastor asked us this question. Among you guys, who is dating any of these girls or guys?

Wow! No kidding. People were afraid to place their hands up to facing the truth. Among the group, Austin look at me and I look at him, then we place our hands up. Then brother Sammy ask the question again. We both told the truth that we were dating. After we answer his question, he told us to go home.

The funny gossip begin to spread. Some friends were like really. You kidding me. She is so beautiful for that guy. Mostly her stander of education is so higher than him. And the gossip was going on and on.

But who cares, we wasn't looking at higher education either. We both were looking at the heart that we both had love for one another and it wasn't fake love but true love those days. Gossip did not stop us from moving on. At that time I was in the SDA School and he had just started going to Calvary chapel school. I was happy that he make a great decision by going back to school.

The incredible part about Calvary chapel school.:

Fun never dies; I which I could turn the page back about this school. Great teachers, and great friends. I miss all of them.

When Calvary chapel school opened in 1995 , I was attending the SDA high school, because the Catholic school couldn't take us again due to our age and the civil war. They were accepting age 5- 11. I was one of the smart students along with my friends Alfred, Sam, Bledee and so on. We were the under rolls students those days in grade 7th.

The reason I left the SDA school:

Due to unemployment, my both parents couldn't pay my school fees anymore. I got a scholarship as a choir members in Calvary chapel school.. There were lots of kids going to school free of charge. The opportunity I had was great blessing from God. Which was great for my parents. Because dad hard so many kids living with him that needed education as well.. And at that time he was paying everyone school fees, so he was bless by me going to free school.

It was a blessing from heaven that passed through these good Samaritans (the Lowe's) by opening school for the poor like us. Things were very tough those days after the civil war.

School fees where very costly and there were lots of unemployment families in Liberia. So must churches open scholarship and were helping many kids to go to school free. The late Henry jr, and Joshua were going to Methodist school while Erika and the rest of the kids were going to Ariba school in Moore town.

Most of us use to walk to go to school. Due to the economy system in our country cause lots of shortest of transportation in the country. So many of us use to walk to school. The good thing about my school, is that it was not too far from home.

School rules and regulation:

We were to go to school on time, look good in our school uniforms, respect our teachers, and friends and make good grades. Our school begin at 8:30 those days. We use to have devotion online before going to classes. Mostly Sis Evon use to lead the school devotion. The following were not allowed in school: smoking, keeping your hair like a female, wearing short dresses, peeing your nose and having bad conduct were not allowed in school those days.

The list of our teacher those days:

It was Brother J's, Brother Flanpor, Brother Daniel, Brother Othello and our English teacher but forgot his name. He was very good at his subject. Brother Chet was our bible teacher. The best bible teacher I ever had in school was him. Not because he was my missionary. To be frank, his teaching was very simple and understandable. At the same time, very patience and good at teaching his student how to read the bible, drop down ideas such as: observation, comprehend and memorize the bible verses during our test or exam period.

I really enjoy those moment in school like studying on the beach during school exams. my boyfriend and I used to go on the beach to study the bible, and our school lesson to successful pass. There, we both make a promise with the bible that we will not have kids by different man or woman. We Held hands and pray and promise each other. I believed it was spiritual.

Family and friends my missionaries were people who were patience in one way to blessed others as well as themselves. And they will never be forgotten by me. As people say , respect those who find time for you in their busy schedule ," but love people who never look at their schedule when you need them.

Life is all about happiness:

I finally took the step and walk through my change. I will like to admit that I was nervous going into my change, because of my dad. But after some time, I begin to be honest with myself and stop been bothered with the things that does not matter anymore. Friends and family, life is all about happiness. So long you make a rightful choice, focus on been a happy person. Be willing to make a difference.

My observation as a member as compare

With the Catholic church:

The St Peter Catholic Church in Buchanan, that I broke away from, use to have mass two times on a Sunday. We use to pray with our rosary. It had a picture of Jesus on it. We use it to pray to Mary and Jesus. It shines at night. I took it as my protection while sleeping at night. Before you get baptized in the Catholic church, , you have to attend the catechism class with a father or sister. Those days we had father john who was our bible teacher. He told us that he had two daughters and his wife. He returned home every six months. The over all priest b wasn't marry at all. And promise not to go back to his home town until death. Very loving . It was fun being with father john when we were kids. Every December they use to share free clothes, toys and new roseray to us and to the less privileged people in Buchanan.

The Catholic church has lots of members and different kind of nationality. The good thing with these two churches, is that they don't believe in dressing like wearing luxury clothes. So I was comfortable been in my new church. some African churches believe in wearing luxurious clothes every Sunday and making their members uncomfortable going to church when they don't have new clothes every Sunday. Jeez! I cannot stand those churches that want their members to look luxurious all the time.

In my church there were lot of respect and love for each other. Everyone call each other brothers and sisters.

Ministering to the community and outside the community to help the less privilege:

One Saturday morning, brother Chet, Brother Othello, Brother Sammy, me and Mardea, went to evangelist in a small town. I can still remember we carry clothes, bible and shower supplies such as: soap, shampoo and hair conditioner for the villagers for donations. They were so happy to see us .They greeted us with love and respect. His donation to the less privileged family, help restore hope and dignity in my country Liberia.

His generosity and good will taught me how to do the same to my country.

Even though I don't have the financial backup , but with my kindness to my own Liberians, and support from individual, the government of Liberia and churches will bring change.

My husband and I have establish a nonprofit organization call Virtuous Women Organization Food Bank in our country Liberia, to help the less privileged family 3 times in a year to break down poverty and crime rate in Liberia.

Your generosity and cooperation as a church, government and individual around the world, will help bring great change to our great nation Liberia. This help will bring change in school and help most kids that don't have the opportunity of carry meals to school . With this great idea, our kids will have a meals to eat and concentrate on their study. Because I went through the same situation as a kid and it hurt a lot.

The Significant of food bank in Liberia:

The significant of having Virtuous Women Organization food bank, in Liberia, is to help most of our singles parents, less privilege family and people with disabilities as well. Most of our single moms will be grateful to have this organization in Liberia because lot of them are going through hardship and cannot afford to fee their kids at home and even in school. I am grateful to get this idea from pastor Chet and this great nation of Canada. Many thanks to their government for helping us and caring for us .

However, I was very impress of his good well.. People he did not know, he show kindness, and had a caring heart for them as his family.

From my house to brother Chet house, was just three to five minute walk when it is dry season time. I could just walk through our little garden in front of our house and go for bible study. It was a red beautiful house with garage and big yard for lots of people to play, study and do lots of things.

Those days, I usually see Saturday during his chores every morning before going to school. While doing his chores, he will be singing gospel music and very happy during his chores for his parents. I really used to admire him been happy to do his chores, and not complaining .At the same time, love was in the air. So funny. They also use to have bible study in front of their house. When it is time for bible study, I make sure I do all of my chores for my parents before going for bible study. During the bible study with Andrea and Ann from Belgium. We learned how to take turned and read the bible as women of god.

It was amazing studying with these women of god from different countries around the world. Wow! What a great joy those days.

My observation for Andrea and Ann was that Andrea was afraid of the sun, while Ann was comfortable with the sun. She use to be indoor all the time when the sun is very hot. Ann use to be with us to play volleyball with us outside.

Brother Chet was very comfortable with the sun all the time. He eats lots of African hot pepper, rice, swallow dumboy as well. Dumboy is our African food which comes from cassava roots. It is the form of starchy food. I believe he was African by choice and American by his compilation. Lol ha ha.

I am grateful today that I met my missionaries all else my plan may have fall into someone else's plan. Thanks be to god for my 3 beautiful kids. Austin, Micaiah, Marcia and more to come by my new husband. I am proud to be call mother. The good thing is that change is part of human nature. In other words, nothing last for ever.

However, the Catholic school was one of the best school I ever attended when I was a kid. Their teaching were different from any other schools. To be frank, they were the best school that every parents wanted their kids to go to. But some parents couldn't afford to sent their kids there Their training were much better for all kids future, that's why I wanted to become a nun

The separation of my parents.

The main character of this book is my parent. Their separation that causes lots of chaos in our family.

When I look back at my life those days, I begin to think about the good and bad things that took place in my life as a teen when both my parents were common law partners when we were kids.

According to mom, she was 16 years old when she had me. I was in her tummy for 11 months before she give birth to me. After she had me, there came Joshua, the late Henry, Olivia Erika, Barron, Decontee Grace, Pious and Hen-Martha.

In addition, dad had other kids outside his relationship which mom took as her own. Our half siblings were the late Henrietta, Emmanuel, Martha-line, Barbara, Diamond, Princess, Daniel, Uriah, Coco-man, Dayou, and U-nawheh. U-nawheh is my dad last born. By his new wife back home.

Here comes family expensive:

Those days every family members from both mom and dad, came to our house for food, school fees hospital bills during those days when dad was working. We were one happy family growing up. Dad had his siblings children living with him, and other people children as well.

We had great time together playing in the yard as family and friends during our childhood. When Dad was coming from work, he usually whistled my name "Tuesday". We would all come running and give him a big hug.

It was fun those days. Those days friends were actually important, especially my childhood friends; Diana, Mardea, Evon and so on. Diana and Mardea had been true friends and like sisters to me since childhood. As well as Evon, they were true friends to me.

Mom was a stay home mom for many year .She was one of the step moms who took her steps kids as her own. Dad was so busy making lots of babies out side his relationship. While mom also accepted some of his behavior by taking most of her steps kids to live with us. Please don't get me wrong, I don't hate my half siblings. But mom also encourage his polygamy idea that is why he makes more babies. If that's was me, I couldn't have go that far.

Well the good thing is that they were good kids that listen to her and respected her when we were living together as family. We all had our own friend, the late Henrietta was my friend, the late Henry was Joshua friend, Emmanuel was Barron friend and Martha line was Erika friend. Decontee, pious and Hen-Martha were little at that time. The rest of the kids were with their moms.

The bad things about too many kids that daddy make outside his relationship, is that he forget about the future and was living in the present until when the future came, it was late for him.

At that moment mom had already have 8 kids by him at the age of 34 years old. And he had about 6 kids at that time by different women who were not living with him.

Separation that shock everyone in our community between my mom and dad:

When mom got employed with the feeding center, the (UNHCR) united nations high commissioner for refugees in Grand Bassa County, mom begin to make good friends and begin to learn some good idea such as self esteem, change her way of dressing and becoming the person she want to be, Dad began to notice changes in mom behavior that she had turned from old school to new school wife. Mom was employed as one of the healthcare aide worker for children that were malnourished during the civil war in our country.

She was very good and caring employee. All of the women that had their kids at the feeding center, those days used to appreciate her as a healthcare aid worker. Even her employers used to congrats her for her hard work towards her own people.

Mom did finished high school because of bearing kids at a younger age. She stop in grade 11th. But she has been a smart woman who learn quickly and very observational. Mom had work so hard in her own country and Canada. I believe is turned for mom to have her own place and enjoyed life with her kids and grand kids.

Whenever, her friends come for visit, they will be telling dad to not treat mom like older women. She should dress good. So funny they were hating on his corn. Which I use to like.

Dad begin jealous until he could not stay at his work place anymore but usually get on his bike and go check on mom during his break time and when he is off work as well. Mom friends were kind of dislike the way he used to be coming back and forward.

They begin to gossip about my dad. And didn't like the idea of him coming to mom work place. Until one day, mom had a day off and she decided to go to her work place for visit to her friends to pick up something.

Guest what took place?

Dad show up at mom's work place and begin to fight mom from the work place until they came home. While they were fighting, my brother Joshua came between them and jump dad to fight. Then our neighbor blazon took mom and hide her in her house. Dad ran from the house and went straight to ma Esther house and punch her in the eyes. Her son Kingar woke up and said that he wanted to fight our dad but his mom said to him, lawyer Kingar, please don't be my lawyer. The God of Sis Martha is the one that curse me. I should have gone to talk to her husband when I hear that they were fighting but instead I stay home and said that I was minding my own business. And she been so nice to me. For this reason please don't fight back son. At last dad went back and apologize to them.

They understand him and accepted his apology.

Dad came home looking for Mom but Mom was no way to be found, she had left and went to her parents house. Dad was so guilty of what he did and begin to cry. He took us to grandma's house to apologize for his wrong doing. But Mom parents told him no! Enough is enough and they all left the meeting.

I was crying and confused. When I looked at my mom eyes, I felt so bad because her eyes were all swollen and red. My question to Dad was, did he forget that what a man can do a woman can also do it? When the cup is filled with water, what happen when it can't take any more, the water begins to overflow and waste. That's what happened to mom. She was in love with someone else, then he got mad and begin to fight her.

When we were kids growing up, when Dad and Mom got into a fight, they usually went into their room. But in 1997 fighting was very bad when Dad went to her work place to find her and they fought in public.

As people say, what makes a man shame, makes him mad. Mom promised not to be with Dad any more due to the embarrassment he caused her.

Dad said he did not know what got over him to go that far and fight mom in public. Years later mom forgave him and we all forgave him as well. We are happy that mom forgave him.

To be frank, mom was a very committed wife and also had self control. Very caring mother in her home. And the community. The community had lots of love and respect for her, and daddy and us those days.

However, when things went wrong, she finally left us with dad after she found out that dad had mentally and emotionally abuse her. I went over to my pastor Chet's house and explained the situation and took him to my mom's parents to help me apologize on my dad behalf so mom could come back home. This was the incredible part base on the story.

I have never seen any man who as bold and straightforward in my life as brother Chet. When he saw my mom's condition, he changed his mind about their reconciling and told her not to go back to the relationship.

If Chet told her to go back to an abusive relationship, and she got hurt or a killed, God would hold him responsible. That was Chet philosophy. He prayed along with Mom and took me on his bike. While riding home, I remember he asked me one question. Ellen! When you grow up, who are you going to marry? I told him that I was going to married a Christian. A man that will love me, and take me, like his mom and respect me for whom I am.

But not knowing, I was referring to his own son Austin. Ha ha so funny. Hide and see love is so embarrassing. But it was secret love because of both our parents. They were too tough on us because of our education. Brother Chet took me straight to his house. I slept there for the night and returned home the next day, because I had to take care of my siblings as the oldest child of my parents.

As the Bible says when you are true follower of Christ, you will love and obey his commandments. Dad wasn't a true follower of Christ at that time when he was cheating on mom and doing other stuff.

How Dad become a born again Christian:

When mom left us with dad, and traveled to Ivory Coast, he changed totally; he became a Christian and join the SDA church. Dad began to have bible study with us every mornings.. On March 7, 1997 my missionaries travel back to America.

Then I began the mom in the house to take care of my siblings. It was difficulty for me to focus on my education and studied in school. Cause I always use to think of mom all the time. She was our everything. When I say everything, I means she use to do our laundry, cook and take good care of us.

Later on, mom sent for our little siblings and took them to Ivory Coast. And left me, Joshua, the late Henry and the rest of my half siblings with dad.

Later, I took off to Monrovia and begin to stay with one of Dad's goddaughter Phelitta. I begin to attendant the Heywood Mission School in Monrovia (Old Road Joe Bar).

While going to school, I had to sell plantain chips with Phelitta on the road at night. Life was so confusing to me because I felt that I have been forgotten by God. Most of my friends of my age was ahead of me . I was down to earth doing chores for them and being careful not to be unfaithful to my boyfriends Austin.

I didn't wanted to break his heart cause we promise not to leave each other. Even though, we did not tell both parents that we were dating but however the gossip spread in the community so my dad heard the news and got mad at me. He said that I was dating a native guy that leave his ears on his head when he sleeps. Ha ha. Funny again. Dad do you cut off your ears before sleeping? I said that in my heart because I never wanted a punishment again. But I believe his parents heard the gossip but didn't show serious concern. As we say in our language they played low.

There lots of good guys that wanted me but I didn't want to show interest because I didn't want to break Austin's heart.

we both had love for on another and promised not to leave each other. We both use to love each other.

For this reason I was unhappy to sleep with any man who wanted to take good care of me. I felt that broken promises can led to depression. and loneliness, as Which I did not want as a child of God, growing up in Calvary chapel church.

My missionaries left with my boyfriend march 7,1997.It took me 8 years more to coming to Canada.

The struggle begins:

The refugee camp life begin. It was like a real life movie. Am telling you the truth. My siblings and I left Monrovia and joined Mom and our sibling in Ghana for the resettlement program for Liberian refugees.

On the refugee camp going to school off and on, I decided to email brother Chet to help me with some money for my school feels. He sent me the money which was $125 US. The test answer was Jesus love you. One of my former teacher of the Dominion Christian academy high school, went alone with me to pick up the money. When we got there and filled in the form, we were told that the money was in cheque and I could not get it very quick.

Well, I didn't have enough money to go back to Accra because it was very costly for me so I didn't go back for the money again. I guess it was returned to him. Maybe not because there were lots of fraudulent act going on in Ghana.

The refugee camp was very tough those days. When I say tough, I mean things were very difficult for many Liberians. We had to be on the internet asking for help from people who we did not know and family members. Because we were doing everything for ourselves. Most of us were self employed. And the self employment was hand to mouth. Our Aunty Josephine and Eddith Capard were great help to us from the United States. They were our breadwinner. I was doing hand to mouth business.

When I say hand to mouth business, I mean for example, I used to sell oranges on the road as a self employed. And it was real life. I used to go to kasoa market to buy oranges to sell on the road with some other girls. If we were lucky that day and people buy from us, we'd get to buy a meal and water to have a bath. But, if not, then we would have to go through fasting.

The sinful nature of abortion:

On the refugee came, I began to date one of the refugee teacher name Browne. I was dating him because he placed my siblings and I on his school scholarship. He was so abusive to me and at the same time very aggressive and always beating on me, whenever he sees me with my male friends having a chat. So I wasn't happy to keep a single pregnancy for him. And these were harmful risk I was taking as a young girl on the camp. One day, I got pregnant again for the same Browne. I was so worried and called my sister Erika (Olivia) and I explain the situation to her. She sent me $50 US to go about doing the abortion. I went with Sis Witta at the mercy clinic and met the Doctor that own the clinic. Before he could do the abortion, he explain to me about the consequences of aborting. And second he told me to be serious for my education. I should have been in the university like his daughter.

He didn't know what was eating inside of me as a 23 years old at that time. If he knew, he would have prayed alone with me, and hoped for the best future for me. As the firstborn of my parents, living on the refugee camp and having no means of helping myself my siblings and mom, frequently depressed me. At the same time, I wasn't exposed those days. I ask God to forgive me for this sinful nature. And I believe he God save me to be a mentor for others. I could have die from doing abortions.

While other were traveling to the western world every day from the refugee camp, we were still waiting for our name to come up for interview. Sometimes while going to the market to buy groceries for the household, I would be crying in my heart and sometimes being angry with God. I would be asking him why me? And at the same time, I would say, wait for your time Ellen.

The fasting and praying on the camp:

Every church on the camp used to have fasting and prayers. Their main purpose of fasting was to travel to the western world. Because of the situation, in Africa. Africa was hell on Earth while the western world was heaven on Earth. Every church used to have devotion early in the morning. From 4 am to 6 am.

Going through fasting and prayers, just to make it to the white man's land, was very tough sometimes with us. I give mom a big thanks for being our hero, for fasting for us all the time on the camp.

Christian maturity looks like laying down your # one freedom for the sake of a brother or sister # love # disciple" (by Chet A. Lowe)

Life is a vapor that appear for a time. Let work together to help each other out along the way.(Social good).

The difficult challenges I passed through trying to visit the U.S.

My family and I came to Canada in march 2005 . We went for our English test to the central Alberta refugee office in Red Deer, after the test I was place in level 3. Later I went to the college and took my test again, and I was place in level 3 again . I felt so sad and discouraged. One day in 2006,why talking to sis Andrea, she asked me what I was doing. I told her I was in school .Then she said what are you taking in school? I lie to her and said that I was taking nursing. I got so embarrassed again. Suppose this lady came on an unknown visit to me in Canada? What would I do with the lies I have told her? It was so sad that I didn't really finish college due to depression. Then my sister Erika and I begin to communicate on the phone. While talking from one thing to another, she mention about my dairy book I had when I was a teen. I realized that I misplace my dairy and didn't know where it was. I remember traveling with my dairy from Liberia to Ivory Coast to be with mom. Going back to Liberia, I forget my dairy. So my sister took it and travel with my dairy to the United States in 2000.

Trying to go to the United States in June 2011 was one of the days I will never forget. I planned to go to the US to visit my sister and extended relatives for her graduation. So I put in my travel document for the states.

I took the travel document to Moses. One of the workers who worked with newcomers, to help me fill in my visa form.

While helping me to fill in the form, we ran out of time, so he told me to come the next day and leave the document with him. When I went back the next day, he told me that he didn't have my document. I was confused. I did not go for the graduation.

After 9 years later I was shocked to see my travel document again. I couldn't understand what was going on and for what reason these things were happening to me. Then some thing came to my mind and I asked myself, is it because of the dairy book Erika is keeping for me? Because she said that Saturday zeegay picture is still in there.

I had told her to keep it in very good condition for me until I could come over to the States and write a book about the unconditional love that we both had in common. I had been so obsessed over this young guy for so long. Until my sister got tired of hearing the same story .

Every time we started up a conversation, I would always bring up the story about this guy and his parents. One day in 2015, I tried adding his parents on Facebook and wrote his mom, but it took a long time before she wrote me. I guess at that time, she didn't know my TY Higgins name. While talking, she ask me if I was in school. I told her yes, I was. Then she asked me what I was taking in school. I told her I was training to be a health care aide and I was doing my best by passing my courses and my teacher was impressed with me. But out of a sudden, my teacher brought up the topic about Africa, and how in our culture, we don't use deodorant. Most of us smell so bad. I told her that it wasn't the culture; it is base on poverty due to the lack of knowledge and corruption that cause most people to not use deodorant because they cannot afford if.

They preferred buying food for themselves and their family, or to pay their children's school fees, rather than purchasing deodorant. At the same time, we African don't have deodorant but we have the country version called juooo. It is use as deodorant in the rural area. My grand mother use to use it and place it on me after bathing. After giving my point of view, she got mad.

However, when it comes to the deodorant issued she was talking about, it is true; many taxi or bus driver in Africa, or carboy (which is use in standard English as conductors, who collect the money from the passenger, before entering the public buses don't use deodorant often.

And other African but is not our culture. Is base on civilization and poverty. I was just trying to help her understand the system in Africa. From that day on, my teacher got mad at me.

A few weeks later, we took a test in the class and most of us fail the test. Our teacher, Kathy, got mad at us. She begin to ask us why, one by one . Everyone give their reason. When it was my turn to state my reason, a Jamaican lady name Tupas interrupted my explanation by telling my teacher that she should go about teaching us. I turned to Tupas and ask her why she was trying to over look me in front of the class. I told her, we are both black, while are you embarrassing me in front of the class?

At that moment, Kathy ask me to go out of the class, all else she would call the police for me. Kathy did not sent both of us home, just me, and ask me not to take my exam. I felt it was discrimination because I was on assured income for the severely handicapped (AISH); that is why they had no regard for me. So I went to the immigration office call (CARE) in Red Deer and met with Jen Underwood who use to take me for presentation at schools, college, other places to explain my story as to what brought me to Canada. Jen wrote my teacher and told me to give the letter to her. Then she saw me crying. She said to me Ellen, don't worry, you already have a career. Back off.

I went back to the school and give the letter to my teacher, and taught she was going to let me take my exam but she refuse. That's how I quite my health care aide school.

I felt it was a discrimination because they felt that I was on AISH that is why they had no regard for me. I believe they were jealous of me making the different because I told them that I wanted to work with the united nations in my country, when I am done with school.

Speaking of AISH:

Being on AISH, is it wrong to make the difference? My handicap is mental and not physical because it impedes my ability to comprehend and concentrate. It all started when I was separated from my parents during the civil war in my country Liberia West Africa. I was sexual abuse by a Nigerian peace keeper, in my home town Buchanan Grand Bassa county. Which I have forgiven .Base on my age in Canada, I have been hiding a lots of my childhood emotional stories. Base on fear and deportation, and it hurts me a lots and cause me to be depressed. Until when I was courageous to write my real life story, then I began release. To add on to that, when I started going through the tough phases of life it led me to, the psychiatric hospital in Canada. I was into an abusive relation with my ex fiance, my kids father. My depression starting when I was sexual abuse during the Liberian civil war. I was selling body wash for my aunt. While selling, the peace keeper call me to buy some of my goods. Due to fear and seeing their guns, one of them told me to follow him inside his room and this is how I was abuse. And due to my parents separation and my teen boyfriend whom I used to love so much who broke up with me when I got pregnant after he left for the states. This is how I got on AISH.

The relationship with my
ex fiance Nelton:

The month of December 2007, is when I met my ex fiance, Nelton Philips my kids father. I had my first son by the name of Austin blessed Taylor, before meeting Nelton. He was born September 26, 1999 in Liberia. He came to Canada June 2007. His father is Clarence Taylor. Who live in the United States of America. When I starting dating Nelton, things were fine but six months later, things changed. I try bearing it because we have already had our first son 2009 who is Micaiah Daniel Philips, he was born January 4, 2009. And later had our daughter Marcia Ann Philips who was born July 27, 2010. But when the situation of his cheating, abuse and smoking habits could not changed, that, s how I made up my mind and quit the relationship 2015,to focus and take care of myself and my kids.

Those days going through stress with my kids dad and not been happy with his smoking habit, and been abusive to me, I some times call the police. When the police comes, my family, his family will place all the blame on me at times. They will say why call police. Never call police let us handle it as a family. These are some of these saying that led me to depression as well. Base on that I sometimes use to lie when the police come because of all the family drama . Because they all use to get mad when I call police on him. So I never use to tell the police that he was doing drugs which was marijuana and drinking high percentage alcohol which was hurting me inside because I didn't wanted a relationship like that. Cause when he take those things in, he become rude and abusive to me.

Then I begin to think on my ex boyfriend Austin and his parents. And felt that I have make a mistake in my life. Because my dad was abusive to my mom as well. And as a kids I never wanted to be like my mom. She went trough a lot with my dad. He was a big cheater who never had respect for mom at all. But mom was just bearing it because of us. So when I was going through the same thing with Nelton, I got so depressed to the extend that I could not focus any longer in life but to give up hope and said that I will like to be single mom for the rest of my life. People always say these couples has stay together for 30th years and so on, for me I will say, how well do you enjoy your marriage or your relationship, not how many years you guys been together. Because some married or relationship, are pain in the butt. I will never want any of my friends or family members to be in that kind of marriage. because is very depressing.

At night, I would sit and cry and blame myself for embracing the unhappiness I placed myself in for 7 years in an off-and-on relationship.

The main character of this story is my mom and dad Martha Capard Dorway and my dad Henry Samuel Higgins. Who separation brought lots of pain and blessing into our family. When I say pain, is how mom struggle with us for so long on the refugee camps. Going through fasting and praying for a better future. And God answer her prayers and we were blessed to come to Canada. And many thanks for my missionaries who were part of our story from Africa. We are happy we escape poverty. No kidding.

The question was will I loose to stay on a current melancholy lie direction? Or will I rise up and pursuer a life of fulfillment and happiness? The ball was in my shoes.

I was unhappy with my lifestyle. I did not like what I was going through. I was confuse about staying in the relationship. At the same time don't always trust what you see. Even salt looks like sugar if you are not sure, taste it before putting it in your food, keep away from people who make you sad.

Being the first born of my family, all my siblings looked up to me to set a great example. But having healthy relationships or a forward – moving education to enable me to have a career, broke my heart .I guess you cannot stop anything that is suppose to happen to you in life.

The year of conspiracy:

The painful part of my story that encourage me to start writing my biography started in June 2015 when we lost our uncle Joe; and July 1, we lost our beloved brother Henry Jr. he was 32 years of age. And we lost my half sister Henrietta in September. She was 36 years old. That's how I finally came to write my real life story and become a writer. Even though I use to love writing, at the age of 16 and got my own dairy, I did not taught it wise to published it. Until 2015 conspiracy. Or you may say tragedy.

I was broken and confused but at the same time I understand that stress, depression, heartache and overall anxiety are human nature. But it doesn't have to be the case for us. We all as human deserve to have best life on earth.

Additionally, the power of passion can lead us to accomplish extraordinary good things and become extremely successful .

Even though I have written, it does not stop me remembering my lost ones. I always miss them and cry whenever I think of them. May their soul R.I.P.

Lies causes low self- esteem

In 2005, when we started visiting Livingstone church, I decided to attend their membership class because I couldn't find my church branch. (Calvary Chapel).While in bible class, pastor Paul asked me what church I was baptized in before coming to Canada. I was afraid to tell him the truth that I was baptized in Calvary chapel church ; in Liberia by my pastor Chet. Instead I lied and said House of Prayers Church of the Burden in Ghana Buduburam Camp, base on the story my family came up with in Canada.

The 1990 story. I was 7 years old. So I couldn't have known brother Chet as my pastor. I denied my pastor as Peter denied Jesus 3 times. It took me years to say the truth because of our family secret. While in Livingstone church in Red Deer Alberta, in 2008 our sister grace and step brother Abraham came from

Ghana to us in Canada. We all were happy to meet them. They fell in love with Canada; they always say it is the best place on earth. Whenever I say I am going back to Africa to stay, they say, Are you crazy, Ellen? Ha ha. Then we all laugh bout it.

The secret of lies has been killing me inside for 11 years in Canada, which causes depression and anxiety in me. It makes me insecure and embarrassed among social workers, refugees and even in churches.

I wanted a change and the change was to be involved with human rights. I wanted to make a change concerning my birth right in my family, and the poor system of birth right in Liberian history.

I ask God in heaven to forgive each and everyone of us that are in the same situation and cannot speak out like my step sister Bendu, who left her daughter in Liberia and lied to immigration that she didn't have kids. Martee who got married to her husband Doctor in Ghana, Then he and her oldest son got deny by immigration. My sister Martha-line Higgins and my brother Joshua P. Higgins and the late Henry P. Higgins. My step sister Jacqueline Dorway. They were the victims of all. Jackquline got denied because of the DNA results. And most of the family as well. Aunty Annie and Aunty Josephine Dorway who left her kids behind are crying for help to the Canadian government to resettle their kids in Canada for better change.

I believe is about time to tell the truth than to live in lies for the rest of our lives and live with guilt and shame until death. I am so tired of sleepless night and bad dreams.

My brother Joshua also has sleepless night because of our brother Henry's death. They were best of friends as if they were twins . They were two years apart but were the same height, so mom make them twins on the Canadian document. They became the oldest kids on the documents; mom make me the youngest because I was very tiny. The situation we fine ourselves in now, is like a dog who tail has been cut off by his enemies. Since 2005, my mom been trying for my siblings to join her in Canada but no way for her.

The causes of prostitution on the refugee camp Ghana:

Because of the poverty rate in Ghana, Liberians refugee camps led many young girls into prostitution against their well. Young girls dated older men, and traveled outside the camp to braid hair for kids, women, and men before getting their daily bread to eat. Not everyone had to go into prostitution on the camp; there were other that use to do braiding for their living. My sister Martha-line would follow my friend Hawa to Accra to braid people's hair for her living. I use to help them whenever they asked me for help.

When I moved to Edmonton, Alberta, in August 2015, things were very tough on me. My friend Hawa got sick. She begin to call me over and over for help, telling me that she was dying and had no money to go to the hospital. Her last words she said to me were, Ellen Ellen Ellen, how many times have I call you? I said 3 times. She said I will not call you again. Only you I was hoping on. And if you say you don't have it, no need of me calling you. Later, Hawa died on the camp. Due to lack of money to receive good treatment, and due to lack of standard health care aide system in Africa. We are lacking of good health care aide system in Africa, because the poor health care aid system in Africa, our cousin Aaron Capard died in Ghana as well. Africa need standard hospital and professional Doctors to safe lives. I fell so bad when Hawa died. I wish I could help her but I was broke due to the lost of our uncle and siblings. And secondly I was paying 1,225 for two bedrooms apartment when I move newly to Edmonton for me and my kids . I wasn't getting my child tax benefit to back me up for six months. My kids dad was not helping me as well. The child tax benefit people said that I was owing them. I couldn't understand all these bad luck. Every month I make sure I pay my rent on time. Because I never wanted to be homeless with my kids.

Over 6 months I pay $8,150 including my damage deposit .As a single moms with two kids. I was so nice to our landlord but in returned he lied to his department that I didn't clean up the apartment. I clean up his apartment very well. At the same time, he took my damage deposit of $800,and requested I pay $500 plus more. But I refused to paid it, because I felt it was unfair to me. Eventually, I was approved for my capital region housing through the help of my social worker Mano and my counselor, who used to come over to encourage me about the ups and down I was going through. Many thanks to them.

Africa is hell on earth. Like what my brother told me on the phone when he was alive. He said and I quote: Ellen, Africa is hell while the western world is heaven. There is no correct justice systems at all. People get kill just for cell phone if they were caught stealing it. Physical and spiritual killing are very common things. Even if you and your neighbors got into a fight, and you said some mean words to them, they either fight you physical, or fight you spiritual by killing you in the spiritual realm. They will do witchcraft attitude to you just because of those common things you and them pass through... I am serious not a joke. Life in Africa is very sad for the less privileged people. Food is very expensive these days. Low-income people are crying and complaining everyday and no one to listens to their cries..People that work in the government make more money, and I don't see any changes for low-income family.

As for us in Canada, low- income people should be very grateful to the Canadian government. Some of us from the third war country are very grateful to be part of Canadian culture and to be the bread winner for our family and others. A lots of countries don't offer the opportunities that we have in Canada.

I am not perfect, but I don't enjoy telling lies all the time. My way of doing things is completely different from others.

The corruption that is in Africa today, is cause by our enemies, our close friends, relatives, family and mostly hostile citizens who enjoyed telling lies all the time. I pray that those who think I am a fool for writing this book will put themselves in my shoes .How do they feel by lying all the time to get what they want and refusing to help others. Especially the African government. Since the 1990 civil war, Liberia don't have stable electricity . People are still sleeping with generators, lamp that use battery and candles. Our country is 172 years old and still no changed.

If I had one wish to change the corruption in Africa, I will like for all those that work in the government that getting $15,000 to 20,000 US dollars every month to gave 35% of their salary to help the less privileged family because everyone deserve a good life as well.

The book of John 8:32 says: the truth will set you free.

The false accusation laid on me at a Value Village store in Red Deer:

One Sunday afternoon, I went with my son Austin to get him some short and a towel for a church campaign. While going into Value Village store, we saw a lady and a guy smoking out side, she was on her phone, talking with someone. When she saw us entering the store, she went back inside.

Austin and I went to the furniture area to look around, just in case he found something he liked that I could buy for him. All of a sudden, this same woman that was outside smoking, and another woman came to us and asked us to leave the store. I ask them, why? Their answer was, that I had been stealing in their used clothing section (Commonly know as doka fleh in Liberian colloquial) English.

Can you imagine these ladies accusing me of stealing doka fleh? These doka fleh are brought in free by everyone in the community including me. I say when bad luck follow behind you, banana and all can break your teeth. I call the doka fleh store from me to you. Which means you bring your old clothes for donation, I bring mind, we buy other clothes from the store owner , and we all donate again. I was so mad and emotional. I told them to show me stealing on the camera. I ask for their manager, but no manager came. While talking, they called the police on me. The police came and ask us to explain. The white ladies told lies on me. Then he ask me to explain. He did not allow me to finish my explanation and knocked me down and cuffed me in front of my teenage son.

They brought me outside the building. I begin to cry in my language saying they lie on me. The police girl was friendly and said to me Ellen, I believe you. Stay calm and take a deep breath. There will be no charges against you. Then they told us to go home.

The next day, I went to the Red Deer advocate news department to explain the situation that took place in Value Village. I gave them my name and my email address.

Then I wrote Value Village human resources department about their employees who told lies about me. I wanted an answer and an apology from them. I mail it to them. Up to this day, they refuse to call me and apologize.

A day later I got a call from Jen that Red Deer advocate wanted to have an interview with me. When I got to the Red Deer advocate, I was place in a room, and waited for a lady named Maryann. Finally she came. She asked me how old I was; I laugh and told her my age is private. However my age in Canada is false.

Then she ask me about the Ebola issued in Liberia. I explain my point of view and the little I knew that caused Ebola. I spoke about needing a clean environment and clean drinking water. This was a spiritual attack. I began to tell my family, but no one wanted to listen to me.

My first spiritual attack, came to me when I was working at taste bakery in Red Deer, Alberta. I told my boss's daughter Amy that 6 years came off my age when I moved to Canada.

She told me to go to her dad and tell him in his office. And I did. After some times, I quite the job. But I used to go there sometimes and speak to them and buy from them. I believe he had me on camera. Because it was his office I went and begin to cry and state my date of birth and month of birth to him.

One day while sitting with Aunty Josephine at her house, Linda came for a little visit. While having a conversation, she began to ask me about my age.

She said, Ellen, how old were you when you came to Canada? Because you were very young. I smiled and told her that I was 21 years old; I spoke in Bassa to my Aunty and said Linda doesn't know I was older then that and we laughed.

I begin to be so angry, lying all the time and not telling the truth. Sometimes I say, God what am I doing to myself?

Sometimes when I go for presentation at the school or to sing, I am actually afraid to explain my true story of the Liberian civil war. How I was a victim of sexual assault. All because of fear and family secret not be revealed.

Because as a 7 years old, I couldn't have remembered everything that took place. While I was actually 11 years old when the civil war took place. This caused long -term embarrassment for me.

Fear can killed! It can make you encounter stress, depression and mental illness. Being a brave person at times can save you and others. However, my observation in Canada, and Africa, are to change some advantages and disadvantages.

It is better to stand up for yourself and face the truth. Others were afraid like me .They all say I talk too much. But at the same time, I believe the truth can set you free.

Because of these lies, I couldn't say I knew pastor Chet from Liberia .That he baptize me in Liberia to pastor Paul in Livingstone Church. So I began as a full member of Livingstone church, and got my membership certificate for 10 years. They were very nice to me.

While in Livingstone church, as a full member, I met my kids father, Nelton through his cousin Aldophus. Nelton used to live in Edmonton. But he move to Red Deer when we both few in love. And started working with Olymel in Red Deer.

When Nelton and I begin to live together, he was an awesome guy who love to cook, and help me do our house chores: laundry and cleaning up our apartment. Later our relationship begin off and on for seven year because there were no good communication. We both were opposite. I was trying to be the holy Mary and he was a play boy papa. Refuse to grow up. Finally we both separated 2015. We were never married. He only engaged me. And our engagement was broken due to many things. If you read my book you will understand why it was broken.

When I got pregnant with Micaiah, the Livingstone church family and friends were so happy for me and Nelton.

The church member planned a baby shower for us at the church while my family and friends planned our baby shower at my mom and stepdad's house.

There were lots of gifts that came from Edmonton that Micaiah used in his first year. The baby shower at the church was very great. Sandy, one of our friends from Livingstone church, told Nelton Aunty Ma Jangar that Nelton and I should plan to get married since we were having a baby. Ma Jangar said that she would discuss it with her son. When we got back home, she begin to speak in her language (Krahn) I could only understand a little. Later, she went back to Winnipeg. She did not come back to the church again.

When Marcia was born, Nelton asked my parents for my hand in marriage. His Aunty Jangar, his brother Emmanuel, Emmanuel ex girlfriend Henrietta came to be part of the engagement. My sister Erika came from the states. The Dorway family came,

my friend Ann, pastor Paul and his wife. Then few of Nelton's friends and his ex girlfriend Dana, too.

It took place in our parents former house which they lost because of unemployment. My stepdad refuse to stay and help mom pay the mortgage.

The engagement took place in December 2010. I still have the ring which I am keeping for my daughter Marcia.

I am a woman of compassion who loves to help my partner, but my partners sometimes take advantage of me and use me like their old lady. And I wasn't old for them.

We were like the same age. my children's father refuse to tell me his age, telling our kids that I am older then him. All I know I can't born him. It's just that everyone came to the western world in different ways. Some of us came with our real age while others change their age because of standard of living. It depend on your story.

If we had not done that we couldn't have traveled to the white man land.

It is more difficult to travel to the white man land than any other countries in the world. This issued has led many people to deny their own identity and has caused many separations among friends, family and society.

The reason I kept my engagement ring for my daughter Marcia:

When she turn 16, I will give Marcia my engagement ring as an heirloom. The family pictures we took during my relationship with Nelton are our legacy for our children to keep, and remember all the good and bad things that took place in their parents lives. Don't make the same mistakes your parents made in the past.

It is better to say the truth to your kids than to lie. Lying is okay at times, but to lie on the day you were born is forbidden in our society, and to your kids.

Therefore, I am asking my kids to consider me and forgive me for my ignorance that caused me and my family lots of pain. My prayers is to spread the good news to those who are going through the same pain I went through during 12 years in Canada.

I was ashamed of telling people my age for many years.

One day, because of the bulling in Red Deer, I began to used my real age.

I wasn't afraid again. I said to myself, Enough is enough. If the government wants to deport me, let them do so. I am tired of eating crabs with shame (which means am tired of shame). I began to let out everything because I felt I was in slavery.

At one point of time, when I was working with tasty bakery, I got tired of the bulling and confronted my manager. I told him the truth in his office. I was emotional and crying. I believe he had camera in his office that was monitoring my moment and told the Canadian government that it was a fraudulent act. I believe he took video reports or pictures to the police and reported me.

As far as I am concern, I am a free citizen of Canada and I only told the truth. The truth shall set me free. I am a winner but not a looser.

Many people may be going through the same but they are embarrassed to tell their story to the government of Canada. When they tell, the truth, the government will tell them it is fraud,

Which will led to not joining their loved ones in Canada or the United States. The way the white people do the whole system of coming to the western world is killing the Liberians.(West Africa) we have to lie at times, just to come to this beautiful country that has lots of opportunity for all ages. our government don't care about their citizen. No one wants to live in poverty life for ever.

I will love to advocate on behalf of my mom Martha Dorway son, Joshua p. Higgins and our sister Martha line Higgins and her grand kids that left behind in Liberia to bring them to Canada.

We are dying slowly in the western world. We can not even save money due to the economy system in Liberia. Things have gone backward in Liberia more than before. Due to the economy system and the civil war, in Liberia, we don't have loonie and toonie anymore in Liberia. This system has make the country so hard for kids and family. Food are so expensive to buy. The less privileged family are going through hardship and crying everyday and night on the Liberian economic systems. The US dollars rate is high up to the extend and causing lot of hardship for the citizen.

Many Liberians, family and friends are looking for the opportunity to come and work in Canada. I will be so grateful when some family and friends are opportune to come and work for a better living . And also when they are opportune to get a job in Liberia as well. My mom doesn't have a place of her own since her son pass away, she has not been OK. She cannot afford an apartment. She is going through depression but she keep it to herself. At time when she think on our brother death, she always encourage herself by saying that she put her trust in God. When someone you love died, you are given the gift of second chances. Their eulogy is a reminder that the living can turn their lives around at any points.

You are reminded that your feelings are not who you are, but how you felt at that moment. Your bad choices defined your yesterday, but they are not who you are, today.

Your future doesn't have to travel the same path with the same people. You can start over. You don't have to apologize to people that won't listen. You don't have to justify your feeling or actions during a difficult time in your life.

You have to put up with people that are insecure and who want you to fail. All you have to do is walk forward with a positive outlook, and trust that God has a plan that is greater than the sorrow you left behind. The people of quality that are meant to be in your life won't need you to explain.

They already understand that being human is a roller coaster of emotions, rain storms and sunshine, sprinkled with moments when you almost reach the stars.

My pray is that my dad must explain his story to people that polygamy is one of the issued that is slowly killing we the African today. It causes financial break down, poverty, hate and fighting in family and society.

Even in the family, our half- sisters and brothers feel that they are nothing. Most of them ending up living in the rural area with their kids; they all lost hope. There are no job and no education for them.

The polygamist that abused me for giving advice:

I had been observing the Liberians community when I notice one guy name Momo was polygamy. Because I told him the truth, he began to insult me emotionally and mentally .

I was trying to give advise to Momo's second girlfriend Janet, who was my cousin Seth's ex girlfriend; she had me on speaker while Momo began to curse my private parts.

He lived in Calgary, Alberta. Most of these Liberian men are playing games with all the single moms in Canada. When they are not smart, they will be single for the rest of their lives. What a shame to Liberian men. They need to grow up and be the men for their own kids. Momo has three babies mamas from Liberia and two from Sudan. He has left them as single moms, and at the same time, one is calming common law in secret and hurting her friends in Canada. The worst part about these girls is that they don't have the self-esteem to prove to these young men that they can still live with out them.

The government of Canada takes the place of father for all these kids that are born in Canada, and who were born outside Canada as well. Without this child tax benefit, these kids will be some things else.

Most Liberian men refuse to provide for their family. Most of them are pain in the butt for girls, even for the white girls as well.

At the same time these girls are afraid to tell the truth. When they say the truth, their child tax benefit get cut off. Like my sister grace, the moment she said that she was common law, her social worker got mad at her. What else do we do in Canada?

Should we be single for ever? Now my sister is planning on getting married as well. She is following in my footsteps and not telling lies anymore.

The older men are following the young boys footsteps; they are also looking for young girls. Most of them are refusing to get their age mate because of benefit. Ha ha funny. My stepdad who separated from my mom 2013, has joined the club.

This child tax benefit is causing lots of chaos in marriages. When somebody you love stop loving you and walks away, its an insult before comparison. This issue has cause lots of damage in marriages, and relationship, because the Canadian system . If you make a certain amount of money, you cannot get these benefits when you are married.

For me I support their system, but others get mad at the systems and cause lots of regret in their relationship. This issue is causing lots of chaos in peoples relationships.

When my step dad started complaining to me about my mom concerning not having kids together in their marriage, I told him to stop worrying himself. for his age, I told him to enjoyed himself with mom by travelling and living life and having fun , but he didn't listen. We are his kids too. Even though we are not his biological kids, but we all love him because he did a great job by bringing nearly all of us to the white man land.i wish I could pay him back with something he really wanted for his lifetime. He really wanted a low-income housing. He and my mom both deserve to be happy.

He is a Decon in Agape ministry his daughter Bendu ministry.

I was once a member in their church but due to unfair treatment towards me, I left their church. As God could have it, I found my church Calvary chapel branch from back home when I was 16 years old through my younger sister Grace.

That's how I got in touch with pastor Dejan on Facebook. He reply to me and sent me the address. The first day, I went with my mom and kids. It was my little brother Pious who drove there.

Since then pastor Dejan has been making sure that I go to church every Sunday with Jackquline and her husband Lawrence. Thanks be to God for these wonderful couples. Even though the distance is about 28 minutes driving, I love my church and it worth worshiping the almighty God. Praise be to God that I found my church branch after 22 years. I am very much comfortable there, and there is no dressing competition.

One other thing is not to lie to yourself. If your passion is to help the poor, like me, go for it, even though I am not rich.

You don't have to be Bill Gates before you donate to the third world countries. Feeling guilty is not living life at all. Go after what you truly love.

I believe without my passion my life will never truly be fulfilled.

I tell my kids all the time to live with a passionate heart, it will keep you safe. My motivation is to teach my kids to be passionate for one another and others. At the same time, teach them to be wise and listen to the wise one too. I teach my kids to tell the truth . Certain changes were hard for me to make until I came up with a specific list that I wanted to change.

Told my kids my real age and my Canadian age.

I set clear goals that I wanted to achieve. I write them in my book so I can remember them.

Base on the advice of others, I made sure the goals I set were good for me.

I distance myself from friends whom I consider to be bad example. I wanted friends who had positive influence on me.

I took myself from physically and emotionally abusive relationship.

I made a commitment to pay closer attachment to my kids .

I tell my kids not to go to stranger house in the community and outside the community.

I decided to read more books .It has help me to become more stable at home with my kids ,rather than going to my neighbor's house and chatting with them when going through a lots those days in Red Deer with social workers for my son Austin and my ex (Nelton).

I am so proud of myself that I listen to myself and my mom, others relative and friends and made a change. Things get easier the more you practice. When I do fail at times, I do not let it discourage me like it did in the past.

I simply learn from my mistake, make changes and move on. I would like to say these changes have made me happier, more successful, and a more calm and composed mother than ever before.

I could not have ever imagined the life I have right now, and I am

Still learning every day.

After all, experience has made me stronger and I love to share my experience and help others.

My mean goal is to travel back home and help single moms and the less privileged family to make changes in their lives and feel better and healthy like me.

Moreover, I have lots of family members and friends that fall into this category. They will need more help and willing to learn from me. Like my best friend Diana; she is a true friend that I cannot let go of. And Mardea, and Evon. We have come a long way. Our parents have struggled with us and I believe it is about time that God has given us the opportunity to become the true light of our families to bring unity and love into our mist.

With unity, we can carry each others burdens.

Like what happened to us in Liberia when my brother died; Diana went there to represent her family and stood with my brother Joshua and my dad Higgins. That's how a true friend behaves.

Diana has been a true friend to me since we were kids. I love her so much. Even when her mother passed way on June 2, 2016,when I was planning to go get married to my husband Valentine, I felt so bad because her mother did not enjoy life at all. All through her life, she was selling chi coal to feed her children and grand kids. My question, is what does the government of Liberia do with our natural resources and its money? And the social assistance money they get from other countries around the world ? And loans as well. To be frank, our beautiful black women and children need help. I believe we can do it as a team to help these people.

Diana's mother was very beautiful. I use to love her way of smiling; her smiling was very attractive. May her soul rest in peace. My pray is that God would guide Diana's dad and the rest of her siblings to see Diana proposing in the western world and live longer to enjoy her help.

I also pray for my mom and dad and stepdad to live longer and see us living good lives and see more grandchildren. I pray for my husband and me to have kids in our relationship and be a happy family. However, our love doesn't come by having kids in the relationship. What matter is that we both love each other.

Praise be to God for the caring husband he has given me. I also pray for my brother Joshua and his common law partner Aba and their children to live long. I pray for them to come join us in Canada. Because it has been 13 years since mom has not seen her son.

Mom has been diagnoses with diabetes so she cannot just travel to Africa like that. She cries everyday for her son that died in our country. I pray that mom get low- income housing like me. I ask the government to help bring her grand kids to Canada.

She is spending too much money on children school fees and food every month. She is not saving anything .All her money goes to her grandkids. There is no free school or cheap school, and school fees are very expensive . The stable food that we eat in Liberia is very expensive ,which is rice. A bag of rice that is 40 kg cost $ 11, 568.75 Liberian dollars. That is too much money for the citizen of Liberia. That is almost $ 100 United States dollars. God forbid. We need help.

I am responsible for one of my brother's daughter in Buchanan, who is living with my aunty Marie. I am paying her school fees every month. My prayer is that they all join us in Canada for a better living.

I also pray for my missionaries and their families to live long and met us one day. I can not change the past, but I can write my story and help others. My second son was name after my missionaries' son Micaiah. It means "no one is like God", From the book of 1 kings 22:1 – 38.

Before my dad could come to the states in September 2014, I got stoon crazy and I was taken to Ponoka's mental hospital. I begin to tell the doctor and social workers my real age and told them my son Austin's father was Austin Lowe. I began to read the bible and began to sing gospel songs as well. I was kept in the hospital for 3 weeks before going home. That was spiritual attack again.

My visit to my dad in Liberia, January 2012:

When I travelled in January 2012 to Liberia to visit my dad, my passport was stolen. I called my mom, and stepdad ,and siblings to tell them the problem. Instead of helping me solve the problem, they made things worst for me. My mom decided to call my siblings in Ghana and say that my coming to Liberia would cause them to fail their interview.

I had no right to tell immigration that I was going to see our dad. Base on the 1990 story, my dad was unknown. I told them you can still find an unknown person since he isn't dead. They all refuse to agree with me.

My sister Erika, who help me buy my second ticket, because my first ticket I bought myself, was fake according to the airline in Calgary, the guy I bought my ticket from was a fraud. Erika began to tell me that I should call immigration and change my statement that I didn't come to visit my dad ,but instead I should say I went to visit family.

I said, "No, I Am not going to do that. Even my own uncle Moses tried to discourage me ,saying that so long as my passport was lost, I wouldn't be able to come back to Canada. Is it a bad thing, visiting my own dad? Or is it because of lies we all have said, causing this misunderstanding? I could not sleep. I knew something was wrong. Then dad called my siblings in Ghana to tell them to forget about what mom told them, and they should not think that I am the problem to their traveling to Canada. Instead, they should embrace me when I arrive to Ghana to see them, because we are one blood. They agreed.

The investigation at the Liberian police station for my stolen passport:

While going through the investigation for my passport, the police begin to ask me and my siblings who was the oldest. My siblings said I am the oldest. They ask the late Henrietta; she said she was born in 79. Barbara said that she was born in 81, diamond said she was born 92 and so on .When they reach me, I said I was born 84. Then they sent my siblings outside and keep me inside . There came this police woman name Fatu; she begin bullying me by telling the police to place me in jail, 'all because I had my legs crossed upon each other.

Fatu said I was sitting on her office chair, I couldn't see any office at all. All I saw was on big room with a table and two chairs. I wasn't sitting on her chair. The chair was given to me by the FBI officer.

She told them to put me in jail. The Liberian jail is one of the dirties jails I have ever seen, compared to Canada's jails . Liberians jail have no toilets.

When I came from out of the jail, I got sick and almost died. I was rushed to my Uncle Jacob's clinic. Thank God for those doctors who treated me.

I toileted on myself and vomited all over the place. I had no clothes on me due to the seriousness of my illness. God save me to tell my story.

I was so depressed. I asked God why they were all saying negative things against me. A week later, my Uncle James, my dad, and I went to see the native doctors about my passport.

The first native doctor told us that the person who stole my passport, wanted to kill me, so I should kill the person. But I refused to kill someone for my passport. We went to the second native doctor; he said that it was stolen by a thief, then gave me instructions. He said after doing that, I would find my passport again.

When I came home, I was afraid and began to pray and ask God to forgive me .I didn't want to killed for a passport. Everyone was saying that my passport was stolen by my friend Evon; when she came over to my house, she told me to be careful with my family members. But I told her that my family members would never harm me.

After she left, my passport was stolen few days later .Everyone of my family wanted to beat her, so she ran away. I went over to her house and asked her ,but she said it wasn't her

My main reason for asking her was that she wanted me to go alone with her and sing on a church cruise with Pastor Reinhard Bonnke, and I told her that the western world doesn't take church business as seriously as Africans. I said she has to change her way of doing things. But she got mad at me, and that, s how I took her as number one suspect.

However, we are still friends. I am so sorry for whatever took place between us, Evon.

My advocate support for my sibling Marthaline Higgins and Joshua P Higgins to join our mom in Canada:

When I came back from Liberia 2012, I begin to experience lots of things in my house. At night I will be writing in the holy bible, I was told to change my son's name from Austin Taylor to Austin Lowe in the month of May. I begin to cry that night, and said, God why is this happening to me? Where have I gone wrong? A week later, Marty Skinner came and asked me to collect all the Western Union papers and Money Grams papers that the church had requested it. I told mom and Grace that Marty had requested the money transfer papers from them as well.

They gave them to me and Marty took them to the church. Then the church call my mom, my sister Grace, and I for a meeting. It was pastor Paul and Deacon George. Pastor Paul asked mom, who is the oldest among your kids? Mom was still lying. I spoke to mom in our language, and said, tell the truth. God said the truth will set you free. Maybe, if you stop being afraid, and say the truth, then they can help bring your kids to Canada. Mom said it has been written by United Nations that I am the second born, so she cannot turn around and change it; then they would deny my siblings. I said Mom, I just came back from Liberia and I witnessed so many things when my passport was stolen. Please listen to me and say the truth. Maybe after knowing the truth, they will bring your kids. She said no. A few months later, my brother Barron went to Ghana to meet our siblings. He sent for our dad to Ghana to meet him. Dad went there and met them. They spent four months together.

After the visitation, Barron came back to Canada and Dad went back to Liberia. Our brother Pious was the next person to go to Liberia to meet our siblings and Dad. At that time they had left Ghana and had move back to Liberia. It was the Ebola Crisis when pious went to Liberia to meets Dad. Pious met Dad, Joshua, the late Henry and the rest of our half siblings and family members.

Now it was the four of us that had gone to Africa to meet our siblings and Dad: Erika from the States, me, Barron and Pious. Every pictures were place on Facebook and mom was still afraid and lying. And the government monitor every moments of Facebook.

The next person that went to Ghana before my siblings could leave Ghana to go back to Liberia, was our stepdad Jessy. While visiting Ghana, he and our brothers got into a fight because he was dating mom cousin. So he got mad and called Mom saying that he was the only person that could bring my siblings to Canada and he was the same person that could stop them from coming. When he came back from Ghana, my sibling were called for their interviews at the embassy. During the interview, they were denied and told to go back to Liberia. When my stepdad came back from Ghana, he told my mom that he didn't want the relationship anymore. That's how he move to Edmonton to his children.

I told my parents that my passport was stolen for a reason. I believe I was documented by the US and Canadian governments to know my real age.

They asked, How do you know? They couldn't see what I was seeing because it was spiritual attack from both countries. Liberia was part of it as well. It started when I was stopped by immigration at North Dakota's US border,

When they found drugs in Nelton's friend Momo's car. They asked us to be fingerprint, and we were told to go back to Canada. They were keeping eyes on me.

When my passport was stolen, it took me years to forgive those who were a part of it, because at first I didn't understand their aim. But now that I have understanding in the spiritual realm, I know that your destiny shall surely come to pass .The voice of God told me to change my son's last name to Lowe.

I send money to Sis Grace to fix Austin's birth certificate for me. I called papa(Marty), and told him that I am changing Austin's last name to Lowe. But he told me not to change his name.

But when Dad went back for my late brother Henry's burial in Liberia, he got two birth certificates from my play mom with my son's name on them and brought them to me in the States.

I brought one to Canada, and I used my Aunty Josephine's address to post the second to Sis Andrea. Before, I did not believe in spiritual attacks, but now I believe that all of life is spiritual.

From what I experienced in 2011-2015, I never new it could have happened in real life.

My brother died on our younger sister Hen-Martha birthday, July 1 since then she has never celebrated her birthday.

Therefore, I am not going to give up on my present lifestyle based on my past. I have released the spirit of fear that caused me disconnect with the Lowes for so many years. I am willing to repair our friendship again no matter what. We are one family in Christ.

I was determined to see them in person when I came to Canada; unfortunately things did not work out the way I wanted. I do believe that one day, there will be a reunion for all Calvary chapel Liberian members to see once again for reflection.

I believe it is going to be great. I am happy that I have come to say the truth instead of keeping this forever, which ate me up with depression because of my age changing to come to Canada.

Lies have kept me back. Sin has many tools, but a lie is a handle that fits all. When I think about all the lies, it is amazing how prejudices kept me from the actual truth.

But when you know who you are, and what you want to do with your life, you will not want to hide your light.

As the bible says, the city that is set on a hill cannot be hidden . The make of a true hero is humility. Life is all about test.

You can hide from man, but not God. He uses someone who has issues too.

Finally, I decided to write about my missionaries because of love. Love is action not invisible in society. It has to be visible to everyone. And second, I was inspired by them to write my true life story that took place years ago to motivate others.

I have been praying for a royal wedding since I was 16 years old, I wanted to get married on my real birthday, and I was hopping to invite my pastor Chet and his wife Andrea to Canada, for my husband Valentine and I wedding, but it did not happen. Thanks be to God that we got our vows renewed, and celebrated with family and friends in church.

I don't have to consult my enemies before God blesses me. I am a winner in Jesus name. Without you lord, I am nothing. You created me for a reason. To make the difference.

I am not afraid to explain my shame and disgrace in public because you are the reason I live among my truth friends.

God, may you bless my family and friends who make me who I am today.

Moreover my missionaries Chet and Andrea. And my parents as well.

L .... Live what you love.

O ....Outside and inside your countries

V ....Value your books

E................................Ellen TY Higgins

Let us love one another because love is of God. I blessed God for my missionaries for being in my life back home in Liberia and the western world as well. Love you Chet and Andrea .

To order more copies of this book, find books by other
Canadian authors, or make inquiries about publishing
your own book, contact PageMaster at:

PageMaster Publication Services Inc.
11340-120 Street, Edmonton, AB T5G 0W5
books@pagemaster.ca
780-425-9303

catalogue and e-commerce store
PageMasterPublishing.ca/Shop

About the Author

Ellen Higgens is a wife and mother of four children. She is originally from Grand Bassa County, Liberia but came to Canada in March, 2005 where she was inspired by the Canadian government's system. She thought it wise to impart the same values in her country in order to bring change to Liberia.

www.ingramcontent.com/pod-product-compliance
Lightning Source LLC
Chambersburg PA
CBHW070028110426
42741CB00034B/2689